Skate/Glove

poems by

Carlo and Nicole Matos

Finishing Line Press
Georgetown, Kentucky

Skate/Glove

Copyright © 2016 by Carlo and Nicole Matos
ISBN 978-1-944899-25-7 First Edition
All rights reserved under International and Pan-American Copyright Conventions. No part of this book may be reproduced in any manner whatsoever without written permission from the publisher, except in the case of brief quotations embodied in critical articles and reviews.

ACKNOWLEDGMENTS

Portions of this chapbook have appeared in *More Than Sports Talk, Another Chicago Magazine, Short, Fast & Deadly,* and *The Rumpus.*

Editor: Christen Kincaid

Cover Art: Melina Mejia Stock

Author Photo: Dennis Sevilla and Tammy Perlmutter

Cover Design: Elizabeth Maines

Printed in the USA on acid-free paper.
Order online: www.finishinglinepress.com
  also available on amazon.com

Author inquiries and mail orders:
Finishing Line Press
P. O. Box 1626
Georgetown, Kentucky 40324
U. S. A.

Table of Contents

Skate 2

Glove 3

Skate 4

Glove 5

Skate 6

Glove 7

Skate 8

Glove 9

Skate 10

Glove 11

Skate 12

Glove 13

Skate 14

Glove 15

Skate 16

Glove 17

Skate 18

Glove 19

Skate 20

Glove 21

Skate 22

Glove 23

Skate 24

Skate/Glove 25

For the Chicago Outfit Roller Derby and Team 110

Skate

You ought to have your head examined. You'll have to, actually. Equipment check: spectacles, testicles, wallet and watch. It marks the start of every bout—more forceful, really, than your average anointing. Knees, elbows, wrists will all have their carapaces pried, shelled joint-guards held agape as if to verify the oyster-soft flesh inside. You will spit out your teeth now—almost invisible, the latest mouthguards—to avoid spitting them out later. It is a private party, you'll be checked against the list: numbers, some of them words (B00M, CR2Y, N0H8, R1P), matched on clipboard, penalty board, arm, jersey, arm. It would make more sense to sing the National Anthem (somebody's sorority sister, somebody's AA sponsor, an all-too-local hip-hop artist with a lot of heart) before the helmet check, but oh well. It will be Ref Furry (yes, it means what you think it does), or Bear Back Rider (that one too) or Two Minute Man (each derby jam, or play-period, lasts two minutes, so we'll let that one alone). Whichever referee you get, he'll stand in front of you and he'll palpate your helmet, gently, hands at your temples, then a bit harder, lifting it, rattling it against your scalp, static building up in your hair, Frankenstein's monster vs. amateur phrenologist. You'll pass muster, sheep-shorn Velcro straps, taped-together elbow pad and all. You'll return to the bench, unclench that helmet, hold it to your chest, superfluously, for the Anthem, pretending you pledge allegiance to any other god.

Glove

Our gym, like all the others, is a single-masted sloop, manned to the timbers by an ardent crew of saw-toothed corsairs, each with their own colorful pirate pseudonym. There's "The Professor," for example, not necessarily a fighter with a laconic and exacting style but rather a writing teacher who spends more time complaining about all the grading he has to do after practice. There's also "Brain" (orthonym: Brian), a former high school wrestler who wonders unabashedly why so many jujitsu practitioners speak "Brazilian." And then there's "The Face"—a Mexican-American Adonis shredded and perfect although he subsists entirely on McDonald's and Burger King—another stud wrestler who we put on all our posters and promotional materials. Of course, he earned the moniker by spending more time flexing in the mirror than training, which ended up garnering him a second nickname: "One Round Rudy." And it is beyond foolhardy to resist a name; they are powerful when unbidden and unstoppable when unwanted. It follows a distinctly high school kind of logic. If some dipshit upperclassman decides one day that you are "Gomez," say, because he thinks you look like the patriarch of the Addams Family, you know full well to accept it with a smile (embrace it even, put it on your team hat and embroider it on your varsity jacket) or run the risk of a baser alternative. If you're christened "The Robot" because you are equal parts long limbs and stiff joints, don't fight it because then it mutates into "Frankenstein" and devolves finally to "Bender"—the hard drinking, foul-mouthed bending unit from Futurama. If you're "Nosebleed," then be the best "Nosebleed" you know how—or "Wolfie" or "Sleepy" or "Danzo," "Weasel," "Johnny 5," "Too Tan," "Keith Sweat," "Sunshine," or "Punch-Your-Mother." Wear it until it becomes you because in fighting there is likely someone who shares that name and is at the ready to sink one more pretender. One day you're the "Ice Man," cold, remote, untouchable and the next moment you're the "Ice Man"—fragile and cracking under the slightest pressure. Best batten down the hatches because one day your colors will burn, or worse, sink to the Challenger Deep splintered by a newer, faster man o' war.

Skate

Abel and Willing, Adamant Eve, Adamn Good Call, Up N' Adam, A'blazin'Grace, A. Moral, Aaron Grievances, Agnus Die, Aversion Mary, Archbitch of Slamterbury, Angel Retentive, Allah Inyahbizniz, Althea N. Hell, Alma Geddon. Back Stabbath, Ben Hurt, Blanch Davidian, Caia-Phatass, Carpe Demon, Dali Ram-Ya, DawnTaze Inferno, Devil or Nothing, Devoida Mercy, Doris Day of Reckoning, Enoch Already. Fall About Eve, Godjammit, Gideon Wheels, Gloria Hole, Guns n' Moses, Harley's Angel, Helsa Wayton, Jehovah Hit-This, Jesus Pieces, Joan of ARRGH, Judas Priestess, Kilty-As-Sin.
Mary MagdaLeanOnya, Mess O' Potamia, Panti-Christ Superstar, Pontius Pile On, PurgaTori, Pope John Maul, Rebelations, Simeon Saturday, Sistine Shrapnel, Skaten Spawn, Sivil Serpent, Sweet Mary Pain, Taint Francis, The Vegan Mary. Amen.

Glove

A fight isn't real until your name appears on the white board in simple dry-erase marker: dry-erase because the fight will most likely be rescheduled many times before the final date is set, and it's never as final as you'd like it to be since most fighters can tell you a story about an opponent disappearing after weigh-ins the night before, or worse, vanishing the day of the fight, never to be seen again. At the moment, the board simply reads, "Rob Sucks" with three arrows pointing for added emphasis, but you know one day soon you will walk into the gym and reflexively glance at the board and there will be your name—your name and a date—nothing more. Nothing more is needed: a name, a date, a fact. You don't know why your throat catches—you knew it would be there. In fact, you have been waiting anxiously for the board to be updated since you agreed to the fight a couple of weeks ago, ever since your coach approached you with the specifics, which in the amateurs never amounts to much. If you're able to find a fight or two on YouTube, you are lucky. Most of the time, the opponent—whoever it ultimately ends up being—is nothing more than a man to meet on the mat, someone who's spent weeks marked in black, or red or green in the grip of your name and a date.

Skate

To watch roller derby for the first time is to experience a passion play of sturm und drang, the metrics of which you might not have a clue. Rare are the sports, after all, where the most popular player is the one sauntering around in an "Ask Me About The Rules of This Sport You Have Already Paid to Watch" (paraphrasing) sandwichboard. And yet I promise you—since I sold you the ticket, right?—roller derby is instinctually understandable. It offers a parable, human and basic. Two teams, in two colors, equal numbers and strength. Two opposing scorers, "jammers," each sanctified with a star. All other players are "blockers"—the jammer-hitters, the soul stealers. Both jammers race to pass this mutinous blockade, "the pack," as many times as possible without breaking any rules, or any bones, or dropping dead of exhaustion. The rest—the screaming whistles, the orchestra-conductor signals, the whole Ptolemaic apparatus of referees rotating the rotating skaters on the track: that is merely the theatre of interpretation, exegesis; the sermon where flawed, mortal action is tied immediately, with bluster and authority, to a choral meaning. With each turn of the track, some skaters are punished, exiled, "boxed" with a gesture like a master admonishing a dog. Others will see their opposition evaporate, "out of play," for being too far from the shifting pack: a cautionary tale of social alliance, avoiding hubris and disdaining sloth. The faster jammer is beatified in a mimeshow of manifest destiny: a referee locks on her, points, and stays pointing, tracing her path as she makes each additional lap through colliding blockers. The contrasting call, "you are not lead jammer," favors a man sweeping useless crumbs from his waist. That first jammer, "lead jammer," wins the purest and most fitting right of all. The mortal right to surrender, exalted; to tap her hips, "call the jam," bring the whole bloody race to a halt, at least for that round.

Glove

As much as I admire Ptolemy's nested spheres and his epicycles as byzantine and elegant as a boxer's angles and half turns, and as much as I love Galileo going toe-to-toe with a pope, the man I remember most from middle school science class is Tycho Brahe—the scientist so badass he lost most of his nose in a duel and simply slapped on another of silver and gold and went about his day. Fighters know about noses; we can spot our own by the obtuse angles at which they often set. A well-placed strike can make blood shoot out in an ion stream or make your eyes water and leave you seeing stars; it all depends on how you're hit. My nose has been broken three times by upper cuts—twice during actual fights. The first time I broke it I stopped snoring. The second time, my nose was straightened statue perfect. The third time it set at a rakish angle, which I try to wear with the same bravado worthy of Tycho himself. My teammate, Rudy, on the other hand, got his nose broken from a straight punch, which caused his nose to bridge and crest like the rim of a lunar crater, but not even this impact could phase The Face's celestial good looks. Is there nothing that can mar that countenance? And then there's Nosebleed, whose nose bleeds every practice even though no one has touched it—some unkind trick of physiognomy. Broken noses blaze brightly, to be sure; audiences hush to them or are brought to anxious anticlimax by a contest that is most likely far from over. It is true the nose can turn almost any conversation to fighting, but it is the least of a fighter's worries. It is much worse to burst a hand, or rip a ligament in a knee or throw out your back. The worst part of a broken nose, by far, is the perfect blooms it sometimes leaves on a rose-white gi.

Skate

We call it "eating the baby"; it is only one of many endemic sacrifices. Have you ever seen Hungry Hungry Hippos? Played pinball? Ever snaked a toilet (thanked god, you had guests in the house, for that saving sucking sound)? You are about to be the marble, the bearing, the once-digested something-unspeakable reamed hollow, fragmented, and suctioned back into an underworld you thought escaped. You have broken the pack off the start whistle, punching between two blockers with your shoulder while dashing laterally to the other side. Pulled off balance, the blockers waver out-of-sync, slight tug-of-war. There is static in their convection field, and you hit again, pummel them, hips churning, squeezing between, shoulders lancing, wedging one foot through. A break: Hurty Gertie falls in the crush, and you overleap her, gain her breach. You are knocked out of bounds by Groper Cleavage, but remain on your feet and rush the diagonal path her own sliding body has opened. Someone else—D-Cup Chopra?—is called to the penalty box. That leaves only one opposing blocker left. You don't see her. Maybe your own blockers have her? Smile: you must be almost through. Except, charging forward, here she is—Ms. No Name, the one you willed yourself to forget, and she awkwardly hipslaps you—tink!—a hit so small, so seemingly ineffectual, your brain offers a sound like one loose nickel scattering to the floor. But because you didn't see her, had all your momentum going in exactly the wrong direction, you wobble, and surprising even yourself, fall to a knee. You are stopped dead, in all that motion and disorder, just for one second, but that second is enough for them to swarm. They eat you up: a pounding waterfall that easily overtakes you—Groper is back, smash!—Hurty is back, smash!—and quickly, so very quickly, you are back with all of them in front of you. The baby has been regathered, regurgitated—you have to do it all again. Welcome to ascension: "He will return the same way you saw him go."

Glove

Every gym has an enforcer. It's not an official position; it's not a sought-after promotion or reward, but it is as inevitable as ringworm. Someone just knows it's their job, like mopping the mats at the end of the night. And it's never the person you think it is. It's not the huge guy with all the belts. It's not the gym star. It's not even a coach. It might be the old guy—a relative term at a fight gym—who constantly complains about hip pain. It might be the woman treasure-mapped in dry-erase marker and with a backpack full of exams to grade. It could be the 120lb guy we can never find an opponent for, or the witty girl who serves lattes at the café next door. If your gym is run properly, you won't need the enforcer very often but when the need arises you will be glad to have one. For example, you might find your gym has a storyteller. A storyteller enriches the class with his entertaining anecdotes during the exhausting warm-ups, while the instructor prattles on about proper technique, and during the tedious and repetitive drills. Or you may arrive one day to find your class has a student teacher. This student's knowledge is so deep it rivals and even exceeds that of the instructor. They offer up a constant stream of critique to their partners and without any thought of compensation or recompense. And then there's the streetfighter. The streetfighter is the unquestioned alpha of the group. He's Wyatt Earp and Doc Holliday rolled into one and, consequently, a much better fighter than everyone in the room. He admits to sparring a bit too hard, especially with new people, but it's his duty to teach them a lesson in toughness. It's at this point, when the patience of even the most sainted coach chokes in their throats, that the enforcer taps the individual for a sparring session. After a round or two (at most), she politely accepts the abandoned pair of brand new gloves as trophies—trophies that will go into the box behind the boiler.

Skate

The truth is, if I were going to have an affair, it would be with you. One of you—the burden of so much choice. The husbands and boyfriends know it; the wives and girlfriends—equal opportunity—know it, too. We can make them Derby Widow T-shirts, chain our new matronyms (Mimi Furst and Hugo Furst; Wholigan and Whosdaman; Smashtag and #girlfriend), make the teenage afterprom argument that just because events take place late at night, doesn't mean there's anything "going on." Cross your fingers—cross your legs. It is simply The Case of The Too Many Bodies burgeoning together, alive. Like joining a tribe of bonobos, where initial contact is to place a warm hand on a neighboring groin, and where brightly colored butts signify a readiness to play. Thighs striated like expensive sushi; thighs dusted with cellulite as light as pocket lint; thighs marbled with the cold of early morning, where you fell, hard, at dark o'clock practice and speckled those thighs with tears while I held the ice—there. But you, you have the body I like the most, finely turned, neither fleshy nor winnowy: compact, square. It is hard to believe that you carried a child (a child snuggled sleeping, somewhere) though I have heard the same said about me, and we both disbelieve it of ourselves—raise our shirts and pinch our midsection skin, point out the barely perceptible maplines, as if they might lead us, only, home. But let me say it, once, aloud: the only thing hard to believe is that you carried a child for someone else, my dear. That for all the tumult and scraping, our limbs blunting, clouting, the mating dance of our bob and weave, cat and mouse, on the track, only on the track—that no fresh life was born, incarnate. What can anybody expect? What can he expect, my husband? We live hard hours in a menstrual hut where we make each other bleed. When I return to my native bed, my husband seems almost rude in his maleness, a roaring, befuddled Heathcliff ready to carve out his Catherine, or sweep her up the foyer stairs. He encircles me, says, "You feel like a little armored tank," and I fall into the melee. I bring him the smell of other women. I die on the sword, but bring my shield to you.

Glove

Behind the cage is a box of broken down, abandoned junk gear we don't like to think too much about: an odd number of mismatched shin guards, gloves with dead Velcro, headgear barnacled and duct taped, a cup no one will touch never mind claim; all in a box by the boiler. It's no one's idea of a treasure chest, to be sure, until the day you catch a glimpse of a glove you once loved or a shin guard you almost didn't buy because you weren't sure you had earned it yet on the borrowed fist or leg of some beginner—their faces flush and bedazzled. They're holding their breaths and gasping, flinching from punches and yet running headlong into them, waiting desperately for the buzzer and hoping to god it'll never sound. And you know—because you did it too—how those first nights will go. The night she punches her husband's sleeping back because she might be done but her body isn't. Weeks, now months waiting for that muscle memory nonsense—just a clever way of forcing one more combination on the bag, one more run up the steps, one more teeth-clattering judo throw onto the mat—only to have her body fire off in sticky sleep. Or the shock the first time he snaps a triangle choke on someone and it catches his partner's face in the act of realizing there is no escape but to tap out or go under. Or the day she runs three miles without realizing it when she couldn't break one no matter how hard she tried before. It doesn't last, of course; training is a grind of its own, but the longer you train, the more of you is in that box worth the sweaty effort of digging. One day, when the fighting is done, all that will be left are the hands, the feet, the bones in negative relief in a box by the boiler.

Skate

It strikes me suddenly, miles into the lap sprints, what the problem is: I'm ugly. That's what it is; the issue all along, so obvious. My body is something horrible, disgusting, a gargoyle, my legs grotesque Flintstone clubs, knotted like turds. That's what's different between me and the girls in front of me: they aren't machines, they stink and strain, I can hear them panting, they each have a skunk-stripe of sweat right down the middle of their buttcracks, yes: but they are human. Meaningful. Worthy. Their bodies are what bodies should be; they step, cross, push, step, everything works together with dignity. While I am a slagheap of white-hot failure: my ribs splintering into pick-up-sticks, my chest a bellows that hums, then whimpers, then screams, a melting Dali watch, weakly ticking. I lash my right leg over the left, throw, throw, stroking in rhythm with the line like a chain-gang oarsman, but every cast (expelliarmus!) is a little short, a little more inadequate, more shameful, then something worse than shameful. Hate is here, and it can't be banished. I'm scratching my arms; I'm burning secret "O"s of false surprise; I'm shitfaced on some floor somewhere, again, drooling at the mouthhole; I'm picking my nose and eating it; the man is heavy on me and he covers my mouth; I'm holding the noose and swaying and trying to decide. I'm losing ground, losing, always losing, and I reach for the chain to the trapdoor that will let down the tears—throw, throw!—and I'm ugly, ugly, so ugly, and that fucker still won't come.

Glove

MMA often disproves that macho line about acting one's size—certainly an even more dubious measure of wisdom than acting one's age. Technique can make a child of a hulking giant, swaddling him down and cradling his once terrifying bulk into a sweet deliquescence that ends in a lullaby and sleep. For that brief moment in the cage or on the mats, the universe is brought back into proportion, makes one remember that absolute sense of right and wrong one had at six when the bad guys always lost, no matter their speed or strength or hideous malice. Of course, one must not fall for the lie that size doesn't matter because it definitely does, and you don't want to find out too late that a two hundred-pound brick-fisted opponent might as well be two hundred pounds of brick.

Skate

Right before it happened, you had a premonition. It was a bad drill, turn-around-toe-stop—stops: as tortured as its description. Legs swivel open and, turning 180 degrees, clack shut with a screeching onto stoppered tiptoes, woefully inadequate brakes. It is hard enough for new girls to do slowly, but we were in a brisk, synchronized line. "I feel like crying," you said, and because it was not an unusual sentiment, we ignored you. I was just retrieving myself from the floor when you pitched down behind me, shoulder impacting first. It was a classic fall. From the Hermès Fall Catalog. I mean to say, there was no reason for me to have paid attention, for those silent ellipsis points to have sprung between us in a trail that dog-led me to turn, skate back, and take your left, still working, hand. There was debate about it, your limp right arm, a cluster of interested faces tapping at it gingerly, mouths skeptical. "It is probably only sprained," a coach pronounced, and you agreed so quickly, "Yes, just sprained" that I wondered if you were really shattered in half, like a sideways version of that joke for tall people, "How's the weather up there?" Since in the conversation we had just held, you had whispered, "My shoulder is broken," and I had said, "Yes, it is broken, but you are all right, you are all right." So ours was a marriage heading to the hospital and not the chapel, resentments already setting in. Close arguments in the car about my driving ("Slow down! Not so bumpy!"), awkward small talk, barely repressed tears. Could there really be so many things malfunctioning—a full ER waiting room, reciprocally indignant—inside so many people in what quickly became the middle of the night? Until finally, and with the solace of morphine, your word and mine prevailed. "Broken!" the midnight orthopedist was almost jubilant, "Definitely broken!" Iridescent image of an arrowhead in the wing of your back, tip of yourself lodged in its paradoxical prey.

Glove

The technique for throwing knees in quick succession is quite similar to the Running Man—that ubiquitous late 80s, kinetic dance craze popularized by crossover rappers like Oakland's MC Hammer. Actually, it's exactly the same. As children in the basement of my grandmother's house, my double-first cousin, Keith and I would create dance routines whose foundation and major content was the Running Man to the hip New Jack Swing of Bobbie Brown's "Every Little Step," or Neneh Cherry's sassy "Buffalo Stance," or even Stevie B's sweaty "Spring Love." Who knew all those weddings we went to as kids in our black turtlenecks (so as to better set-off the gold chains) layered beneath our matching V-neck sweaters, which cleverly rhymed with our gold-tipped dress shoes and pegged, knockoff Z Cavarichi parachute pants, would come so in handy later in life. If only I could find the practical applications hidden in the Hully Gully or the Electric Slide—find the missing steps to bridge the dance floor and the cage door.

Skate

When the bout is going badly, nobody wants to wear the star. Star on the helmet, mark of the jammer, signet of the scorer—you'll get the most pictures, speed-swooping each clear slice of track like Dorothy Hamill, so there's that. But that one-half a glorious solo lap involves, of course, the clotted, horrible portion—coming up again each time you succeed, like a Facebook friend with violent schadenfreude—where you are the pack's punching bag. In theory, we all want to do it—jammer stars march our socks, our sleeves (cloth and inked), wink out from behind an ear, strobe that soft spot dead in the center of the back of the neck, where no gear can protect your motor neurons, your integral stem. Hell, I've even got a winter hat I forced my sister to knit, a longjohns star panty (what we call the helmet covers: intimacy turned lewdly inside-out) in cable and purl. But now that the score is 200 to some two-digit number that, like the end of vital phone numbers, memory wants to transpose, the situation is different. Regular jammers, the good ones, begin to malfunction, throwing bolts ("Equipment failure!") like their toe stops had ejection triggers. Backup jammers, back away. Run that pull-list from acme to zenith, nobody wants that halo—shark bait—on their head. When the bench coach hands the star panty to you—looking not at you but a little past your shoulder, with a shrug to the general universe like, here goes nothing—it will be a sad item, already soaked wet, not in any immediate way, although the last jammer's helmeted head, now pinched between her knees, is still steaming. Wet like a tack blanket from a horse beaten to death in the long 18th century—something like that. Drooping in your very own hand, five points in desperate need of a boob job. And when you hand it over again, two minutes later, you'll be seeing stars—shooting ones, lightning bolts, the sick white-and-grey pulsing of your overthrottled optic nerve. You'll return it, skidding on one knee, humbled, face downcast, a penitent, which you are.

Glove

The real test of a fighter's resolve happens back stage while waiting his turn. Some prefer to fight right away, others need the time to relax and focus. Usually I am openly and unabashedly almost dramatically nervous—so nervous my parents would call it "nerves," a not-so-subtle euphemism for emotional instability—so the longer the night goes on the worse off I am. It is tedious to have to interrupt hand wrapping, pad hitting and teammate bolstering to make frequent trips to the toilet, especially while wearing MMA shorts—which have vertical and lateral Velcro straps plus laces—and then there's the cup to deal with. And there is often a line of other dudes trying to look calm while simultaneously avoiding the nervous talking that sometimes overcomes new fighters. Every fight was like this, except, that is, the first one. For this fight, I wasn't nervous at all. I was bored, ready to be done, unconcerned like I was in line at the grocery store. It wasn't confidence, I don't think. If you'd asked me how I was feeling, I would probably have shrugged. All night, I could hear narration, a voice-over louder than my coach's instructions. I nodded at the correct moments, not really following along but not confused either. The desired outcome was clear even if the steps were lost. Maybe I was too old to be embarking on a fighting career, but I knew what it was like to perform under pressure. I had been a pitcher as a kid, always getting picked for the second-to-worst team—teams so bad that if the ball left the infield, it was at least a triple and probably an in-the-park homer—and yet I did manage to win a game or two. In high school, I was a tennis player better known for my screaming tantrums and racquet throwing than for my skills on the court. I wasn't the kid who ripped his team shirt Hulkamania style when he lost a match, but I was close enough. I knew how to perform under pressure and I knew how to crack under it too, but here I was waiting in line, cashing a check or making a money order for the groceries like my parents still do on Friday nights.

Skate

She is tiny—short, even by our standards, where proximity to the earthly glue of all those conjectural gravitons isn't a bad thing. But not just short—tiny, slinky—one wispy cocktail straw jammed in a barroom bucket of pretzel rods. Mental note of the waitress whip that would—swish—wipe her away. She mulls an appropriate derby name: Teeny Meenie, Slimmy Hoffa, La Petite Mort? Finally she settles on Flutter: sting like a butterfly, that kind of thing. But like all new skaters, she's not exactly light on her feet. There's nothing more mistakenly giraffe-like than a really small new skater tripping predictably over her own unfamiliar hooves. Like God was practicing giraffes in arthropod scale model before he got them right. So she's Flutter, and her call sign—the jersey number the refs will bark, the announcers will intone, the program will inevitably misprint—is X0X0. A kiss to the universe—an air hug, squared. Insubstantial, in a sport where brunt is everything, gunnysack meets flatbed, shotput kisses sandbag. But creation clockworks on, and the rough beasts of Fresh Meat rise, over the succeeding months, from their nattering legs. Flutter is hardening, muscles clipping on the way scissors sharpen a paper doll. She doesn't, actually, flutter—she beats. Not wings: the beat of a hot carotid. A determined, steely tide that brings her, churning, at our backs again and again and (jesus, really?) again. Until one day, I clear the pack, gain lead jammer status, crane my neck behind (uh-oh!) and call off the jam, all without noticing my bench coach twirling the go-hand—Shari Lewis sans Lamb Chop—for me to continue around. It is only a scrimmage, so I can take the extra time to make my lapse worse, more obvious. "There wasn't going to be time for a pass, the other jammer was right behind me!" His eyebrows raised. "It was Flutter jamming, right behind me, and she's gotten so good!" Mmmm-hmmm: unforced error, ancient history, please move along. But a considering cast of his head, there at the last, before the dismissal. It was Flutter, the Immaculate Heart, and really: she's gotten good.

Glove

I don't remember walking out to the cage. I don't remember what song was playing. I don't remember the cage door locking. I remember the bell ringing and then getting hit with a wild right. It was a really lousy punch, yet he caught me on the temple and then the mat began to tip towards my ear. And, for some reason, instead of defending myself I'm thinking about the standardized test I took in second grade where I misread the word, "sweater" as "sweeter." The whole time I'm reading about this kid's new sweeter that he ultimately leaves at the park or something, and I have no clue what is going on. I don't even know what the test is for. I'm just following along, filling in little holes, and thinking about the seesaw balancing record my best friend Craig and I are going to break at recess. It's at this point that I became vaguely aware of my opponent trying to choke me. A couple of weeks after the test, my teacher tells me I should go to this special room where Craig and I would prepare presentations on space shuttles, write papers about California condors, and perform sandwich-bag puppet shows like the Three Billy Goats Gruff for the kindergarten and first-grade students. And I could read all the books I wanted instead of copying sentences off the board. The choke got tighter. If he blew out his arms on this choke attempt, he'd be left with empty sweeter sleeves, waving to no effect like those one-legged air dancers car dealerships were so fond of. The choke, however, was dangerously tight now. Some part of me was aware of being in trouble; I got the gist but by the time I made the move to get out, it was too late. And then I'm waking up.

Skate

Everyone loves a penalty box vacation. The chance to stretch your screaming legs ("Not in the ref lane, D0A!"), tilt your head back ("D0A, do not remove your helmet!"), get some sun. Was it worth it, what you did? She did back-block you, Leggy Phlegming— her forearms against that old trampstamp you got in college amounted to a push, even if it was true, you didn't 100% totally need to fall down. That hit after the whistle ending the jam felt good, all the more so because the other girl was so surprised. Some people pay good money in dark nightclubs to trip like that. Anyway, the company is usually good. There are no stool pigeons, nobody in for cop killing or child molesting, and we've already all been, by mutual consent, getting it up the ass. You can ask how long you are in for ("30 more seconds, D0A") as many times as you want, and probably will, comparing arithmetic ("I've got 23 seconds, I think, you have 17") like longtimers in the rec yard shooting the bones. Re-entry, of course, takes a little more finessing ("5 seconds, D0A, you may stand"). You hold yourself erect: motionless but eager, at your most winning, a tenth-grade suitor poised before that doorbell, wilted flowers at your side. You need to make it up to them; you need to enter, cape flying, like Mighty Mouse, here you come to save the day! Bust up that wall, take that jammer by the hand, whisper that you mean it this time, sweetheart, you've really changed, you promise—but nobody will actually make you say you're sorry.

Glove

He walked in but not out. I was calling the fights that night because I had broken my right hand a couple of weeks earlier getting ready for the finals of the 2011 Team Challenge. Our team went up 2-1 quickly. "The Mechanic" stopped his overmatched opponent in one round. "Too-Tan" was in a dogfight until he caught his opponent's chin with a knee that blanked him in round 2. "No Mercy," sadly, pled for clemency after running out of gas in a fight he was dominating. All we needed to do was win the next fight. If this had been a movie, they would have won match four and it would have come down to an insane Rock 'Em Sock 'Em robots finish with the good guys snatching victory with only seconds on the clock. But that is not how it went. This would have been my fight if I had not hurt myself punching "the Face" in the face. It was clear right away that Rudy's wrestling was too much for this kid. Barely a minute into round 1, Rudy catches his back in a standing rear naked choke, and it's all over. If Rudy catches you in the first round, he's a finisher—the other reason we called him "One Round Rudy." Although a dominant position, having to ride piggyback requires stamina—something Rudy doesn't have a lot of. Maybe it was the pressure of the moment, or his earnest desire to keep his team in the tournament, or just a lack of technical understanding—whatever the reason—it would be both his last day as a competitor and mine. When he bent over, as if bowing to the audience (as if making a grand exit) trying to illegally spike Rudy on his head, he forgot to take into account that Rudy's center of gravity and his own were not in line. When he passed the midway point of his bend, gravity took over and then there was no way to stop the meteoring to the canvas. He landed right in front of my commentary position, his head twisted in an acute angle under Rudy's weight. He didn't get up—not right away, not after the paramedics came in, not ever.

Skate

It is 11 or 11:30 or midnight, and somewhere—in an unloaded warehouse, in an empty airplane hangar or auto-body garage or night-blackened civic arena—derby girls, drenched as otters, live-wired from exertion and adrenalin, are coming off shift. "When do regular people exercise?" they are asking earnestly, stretching in pools of light where bats and moths circle. "If it wasn't late nights, I swear I'd never find the time." They are filing themselves into the starlight, savoring the comparatively fresh air broadcast by 3rd shift at the dogfood factory down the road. They are disbursing into ragged carpools, decamping to the pithily named Late Bar, where the clients are few, but the tacos are many. They are—the instant their skates are off—discussing themselves on Facebook. They are thinking of their roommates and clean sheets, and praying for an unoccupied shower.

Glove

The most important part of the fight is the ride over. Long before the sweaty walk-in music, long before the constant trips to the bathroom is the ride in a down-and-out and duct-taped Ford Explorer on its last legs but tempered like a kickboxer's shins. No menacing opponent's face, no worst-case scenario looms larger than your coach's voice as he becomes the dad you never had—even if your father had been man enough to do his job without complaint or promise of return. The talk never varies and you are surprised to find adventure is not really the color of blood, nor is it the dark of the sea or the lure of distant lands, but a series of sweet platitudes long since memorized and unremarkable in every way, as unremarkable as the back seat of that bruise-blue Explorer where your problems were always serious, always solvable but never small.

Skate

Blisters; bad announcing ("Another great jam by The Big, err, LeBOOBski!"), leagues who smear arcane substances, soda syrup, Gold Bond, bong water, whatever the hell that is, in a doomed effort to make slippery floors less slippery; "that guy" in the self-made Lego body armor holding a sign with your name; botching a star pass ("The Pivot is eligible to obtain Jammer status by retrieving a dropped Jammer panty unless the Jammer is in the penalty box, in which case the Pivot will not be considered the Jammer until the original Jammer…"); walking by a rotting compost bin behind a restaurant and involuntarily thinking, "who here plays roller derby?;" people asking you, in all innocence, what kind of parade it is and when it starts, when you thought you were wearing regular clothes. Ghost points; a really satisfyingly messed up X-ray, the first time you jump the apex (whether you land it or no); screaming whatever you want, "Atreeeeeyu!," "Ou sont les neiges!," "I'm on your team!" (you are not), in the heat of battle; Skater First toilet signs; unearned street cred; saying, "roller derby saved me" and knowing that it's true.

Skate/Glove

There's that roguish streak in her hair—an awesome color a boy like him couldn't even name; it flashes wild like the way she hit his arms hoping they'd just fall off: hers or his, she wasn't quite sure. He knows more about her knuckles than he does about her mother, or father, or whom she kissed first in some car out back somewhere. And that's how it is . . . the moment before a punch lands when it seemed like the best idea—and maybe it was. Most people gave in before getting passed her hip, vintage clothes and through to her perfectly-executed bum. One can't use a word any sharper than that for the way she looks in a dress. His wife, on the other hand, has no bum but an ass, perfectly toned from hours at the vanguard of the roller derby track. On Tuesdays, after beating the crap out of each other at kickboxing class, they'd go home—sometimes bloodied and bruised, always sore—and he'd skate that curve up his wife's lower back gripped like Brad Pitt in *Mr. & Mrs. Smith* after they shot the house full of holes and woke up the neighbors. Their excitement, by this point, may be experienced but it isn't self-righteous; however, it does not work for free. And then they'd laze about exhausted to replay the punches they took, the kicks they threw, who they wanted to take out, and who they wanted to take home. It was no surprise that they were often one and the same.

Carlo Matos has published eight books, including *The Secret Correspondence of Loon & Fiasco* (Mayapple Press) and *It's Best Not to Interrupt Her Experiments* (Negative Capability Press). His poems, stories, and essays appear in such places as *Iowa Review, Boston Review, Another Chicago Magazine, DIAGRAM,* and the *Gavea-Brown Book of Portuguese-American Poetry*, among many others. Carlo has received grants from the Illinois Arts Council, the Fundação Luso-Americana, and the Sundress Academy for the Arts. He is also a recent winner of the Heartland Poetry Prize from New American Press and the Slash Pine Press Winter Prose Chapbook Contest. He currently lives in Chicago, IL where he is a professor at the City Colleges of Chicago and a teaching artist with the Rooster Moans Poetry Coop. A former fighter, he now trains and coaches cage fighters and kickboxers. After hours he can be found entertaining clients at the Chicago Poetry Bordello and writing poems on demand with Poems While You Wait. He blogs at carlomatos.blogspot.com. Follow him on Twitter @CarloMatos46.

Nicole Matos is a Chicago-based writer, professor, retired roller derby skater, and special needs mom. She is the author of two additional chapbooks of poetry: *Oxidane* (BlazeVox Books, 2014) and *The Astronaut's Apprentice* (Dancing Girl Press, 2015). Her work has appeared in *American Short Fiction, The Rumpus, Quiddity, Salon, XOJane, The Classical, The Hairpin, Chicago Literati*, and many others. She has written about higher education for *The Chronicle of Higher Education, Inside Higher Ed, Vitae,* and *Pedagogy Unbound,* and about special needs parenting for *Hip Mama, Full Grown People, Brain Mother,* and *Monday Coffee.* Follow her on Twitter @nicole_matos2.

www.ingramcontent.com/pod-product-compliance
Lightning Source LLC
Chambersburg PA
CBHW060227050426
42446CB00013B/3202